Freeriding and Other
EXTREME MOTOCROSS SPORTS

by Elliott Smith

CAPSTONE PRESS
a capstone imprint

Edge Books is published by Capstone Press,
an imprint of Capstone.
1710 Roe Crest Drive
North Mankato, Minnesota 56003
www.capstonepub.com

**Library of Congress Cataloging-in-Publication Data
is available on the Library of Congress website.**
ISBN: 978-1-5435-9003-6 (hardcover)
ISBN: 978-1-4966-6608-6 (paperback)
ISBN: 978-1-5435-9007-4 (ebook pdf)

Editorial Credits
Anna Butzer, editor; Cynthia Della-Rovere, designer;
Kelly Garvin, media researcher; Katy LaVigne,
production specialist

Photo Credits
Alamy: Cavan Images/Mike Basher, 7, DuncanImages, 11, Henadzi Pechan, 25; iStockphoto/djjohn, 27, 29;
Newscom/MARTA PEREZ/EFE, 5; Shutterstock: Edu Silva 2ev, 15, Geraino812, cover, backcover, 9, Maciej
Kopaniecki, 18, Max Bertolini, 22, Monica Garza 73, 21, OcMaRUS, 17, Teemu Tretjakov, 13

Artisitic elements: Shutterstock: Edu Silva 2ev, nattanan726, pupsy

All internet sites appearing in back matter were available and accurate when this book was sent to press.

Printed and bound in the United States of America.
PA99

Table of Contents

CHAPTER 1

Riding Around the World

As one of the world's best motocross riders, Ronnie Renner has won many awards on his bike. He began competing in the X Games in 2001 and has ridden in numerous moto events. But he missed the natural beauty and freedom to ride when and where he wanted. That's why he decided to cut back on competitions to explore nature on two wheels. Freeriding gives Renner the chance to ride at amazing locations without worrying about times or scores.

One of Renner's biggest bike trips took him to Ocotillo Wells, California. This desert area features unique riding **terrain** and large sand dunes. In between two of the biggest dunes is a 110-foot (33.5-meter) gap no rider had ever cleared. Renner had been thinking about making the jump for 10 years when he decided to try in 2014.

terrain—the physical features of a piece of land

Ronnie Renner performs at the X Games in Barcelona, Spain, in 2013.

Vroom-VROOM! On the day of the jump, the revving of Renner's bike broke the silence in the desert. After one final rev, Renner took off toward the first dune. While airborne, he twisted his bike and body fully sideways before landing smoothly on the other side. Renner became the first person to pull off the difficult Ocotillo Wells jump. It was another impressive feat for the eight-time X Games gold medalist.

"On that jump, I don't know where I'm going to land and how hard I'm going to hit," said Renner. "But you never know until you drop the hammer and get after it."

Ronnie Renner jumps over a sand dune in Ocotillo Wells, California.

CHAPTER 2

What is Freeriding?

In freeriding there are no rules, no times, and no courses. Freeride motocross is about exploring nature and developing creativity while riding. The athletes who participate in freeriding all have backgrounds in various motocross sports. But the big difference is that during freeriding, they can do what they want without any **regulations**. The athletes who freeride like to push the limits of their bikes without being judged or timed.

regulation—an official rule
obstacle—something that gets in the way or prevents someone from doing something

Instead of riding alongside dozens of other racers, freeriders create their own paths. And instead of winning races or competitions, the main focus is having fun. Since they aren't being scored, freeriders can take time to work on special tricks and tough moves. Athletes study the natural environment and figure out how to use **obstacles** or jumps to their benefit. For example, a rider can use a small log to learn how to perfect a rear-wheel bounce.

Freeriding is mostly about creativity and skill.

Of course, freeriding isn't possible without a good bike. Athletes use the same motorcycles used in motocross. These light bikes have a single-**cylinder** engine. They also have a strong **suspension** to help riders land jumps. Suspensions are springs that help absorb the impact when landing. With strong suspensions, riders can take on challenging jumps without fear of damaging their bikes. The bikes usually have a long, flat seat. It helps riders shift their weight during tight turns.

cylinder—a hollow area inside an engine in which fuel burns to create power

suspension—a system of springs and shock absorbers used to suspend a vehicle's frame, body, and engine above the wheels

Many motocross athletes ride lightweight bikes because they are easier to control.

In freeriding, just about any area of land makes a good course. Death Valley in California and the Hatfield-McCoy trails in West Virginia are two great locations for freeriding. Since riders can also create courses themselves, cleanup and care are important. Athletes treat the environment with respect. They do not litter or damage the racing area.

Visual Glossary

gloves
Gloves protect an athlete's hands. They also keep hands warm and help the rider grip handlebars.

body armor
No matter if an athlete is a freerider, trail rider, or enduro rider, body armor is an essential piece of gear. It helps protect the chest and back from injury.

knee pads
Knee pads are often lightweight and flexible. They protect a rider's knees.

boots
Boots protect shins from impact, help stabilize ankles, and can prevent knees from rotating incorrectly.

helmet
An athlete should wear a helmet made specifically for motocross. Helmets should have a snug fit, chin protection, and a visor.

goggles
Goggles protect a rider's eyes from wind, dirt, water, and mud. They should fit comfortably under a rider's helmet.

motorbike
Freeriding motorbikes have smaller engines, are lightweight, and have tires designed for off-road riding.

CHAPTER 3

Motocross

The sport of motocross traces its history back to England in the 1920s. It came to America in the early 1970s and quickly became popular with riders and fans. The basic definition of the sport is a motorbike race in an enclosed, off-road **circuit**. There are many types of races and classes for different types of bikes.

Motocross races are separated by classes, usually 250cc or 450cc. The "cc" refers to the amount of cubic centimeters inside the engine for fuel and air to mix. A 250cc engine has less space than a 450cc engine. So 250cc bikes are lighter and easier to turn, but they're not quite as fast as a 450cc bike. For more power and to ride on tracks with sand or wet soil, a heavier 450cc bike is better. Some athletes ride different bikes depending on the track conditions.

Motocross races take place outside of a stadium.
A course can be made on many different types of terrain,
including sand, soil, and gravel.

circuit—a series of races that leads to a single championship

In motocross events, each class competes in two races. The winner is determined by the rider's finish in both races. A great first race and a bad second race may equal a loss if another rider is more consistent. The AMA Motocross Championship is the biggest series in the United States. There are 12 events a year, and the rider with the most overall points is crowned champion. Over the years, bikes have gotten better, so the races have gotten faster, with bigger obstacles and tougher tracks. The higher quality bikes with more stability allow athletes to tackle these rougher races.

Freestyle Motocross

Motocross athletes looking for more thrills have started participating in freestyle events. There, riders are rewarded on how well they can perform tricks and get big air. Freestyle has judges who look at style, difficulty, and originality to come up with a winner. Tricks include the coffin, where riders extend their legs in front of the bike and lean back. A whip is when the rider swings the bike to a 90-degree angle from his body. Legendary rider Travis Pastrana is famous for his amazing freestyle feats.

Athletes participating in supermoto races ride on dirt and pavement.

Other sports have developed from motocross. Supercross has off-road bikes on an artificial dirt track with huge jumps and ramps. These races are usually held inside baseball or football stadiums. SuperMoto mixes dirt racing, motocross-style jumps, and riding on paved roads. Quad Motocross is racing through jumps and obstacles on an all-terrain vehicle (ATV).

CHAPTER 4

Enduro

Athletes who participate in enduro aren't looking for a quick race. These events are timed competitions that feature obstacles and challenges similar to motocross. The big difference is that enduro events can take days to complete! Some championship events can be 125 miles (200 kilometers) long.

There are two types of enduro races: traditional and restart. In traditional races, riders go off in groups at a certain time and must arrive at **checkpoints** on a schedule. Athletes aim to get to each checkpoint as close to the assigned minute as possible. If riders arrive early or late, they are given a penalty.

In order to get to some sections of the race, riders must go across paved roads. Some enduro riders adjust to this by putting mirrors, turn signals, and headlights on their bikes.

checkpoint—a place along the route of a long-distance race where the time for each competitor is recorded

Some athletes don't like the traditional **format** because it can be difficult to master the time elements. The restart races have grown in popularity, especially in the United States. Riders can go as fast as they can until the next checkpoint, without worry of penalty. If they get there early, they just wait until the next section begins. This format is simpler and easier to score.

Hard Enduro

All enduro is tough, but hard enduro races are for the most extreme athletes. Difficult terrain, rough weather conditions, and tough obstacles are part of each course. To compete in hard enduro, riders must be skilled in all motocross forms. Even very skilled riders can have difficulty completing a hard enduro course. Racers often fall, and sometimes fans will lift them off the ground to help them finish a section. Obstacles include mud pits, river crossings, steep hills, and rock beds. Races take place all around the world, including the five-day Romaniacs event through the mountains of Romania.

format—the shape or style of something

CHAPTER 5

Trial Racing

Despite its name, trial racing is not a race at all. Instead of speed and strength, **finesse** is what makes a good trial race. Riders carefully navigate their bikes over tough terrain without touching their feet to the ground.

Courses contain boulders, tree trunks, rocks, streams, and other obstacles. Athletes move through sections trying to score as few points as possible. If a rider touches the ground for support, it is called a **dab**. Dabbing could result in one to three points added to the rider's score. Riders are also penalized for getting off their bikes, going out of bounds, or rolling backward.

Trials are a test of skill. Riders often look at the course before beginning to form a **strategy**. They can take as long as they want to finish the course. Getting through a section without touching the ground is called cleaning. Trial racing is excellent training for motocross riders of all disciplines because of the skills needed to succeed. Control, balance, and **traction** play a part in all motocross racing.

Athletes in trials use smaller bikes with specially modified engines. These engines are designed for **torque**, a twisting ability, rather than power. The bike's light weight helps with balance and **agility**. Another unique aspect of trial bikes is that they don't have seats. Most riders don't sit down during competitions, and the missing seat helps make the bike lighter.

finesse—great skill or style
dab—the act of a rider touching the ground with their foot for support
strategy—a careful plan or method
traction—the gripping power that holds a vehicle's tires to the ground
torque—a force that produces or tends to produce rotation
agility—the ability to move fast and easily

CHAPTER 6

Moto Games

There's a lot of excitement to be had racing and jumping on a motocross bike. But some athletes have come up with even more ways to enjoy their bikes with moto games. These unique twists on racing started small but have grown as others have discovered the fun.

Motoball is popular in Europe, where it has been around since the 1930s. The sport is basically soccer with motorcycles! Participants ride 250cc motorbikes that have been lowered, and they steer an enlarged soccer ball toward a goal with their feet. Only five players from each team—four riders, and a goalie—can be on the field at once. Similar to soccer, only the goalie can touch the ball with his or her hands or arms. The Pro Motoball Championships are held each year, with France, Germany, and Spain participating.

The unique game of Motoball tests a player's ability to ride, as well as their strength and balance. The rules of motoball are very similar to regular soccer.

Moto gymkhana is another unique way people have fun on two wheels. Originally started in Japan, the sport is an obstacle race that also builds valuable bike skills. Competitive gymkhana events are timed trials during which riders attempt to bike through the course as fast as possible. The obstacles include 360-degree turns, **slaloms**, and tight corners. They test a rider's ability to **maneuver** at slow speeds. Balance is an important aspect of gymkhana. Since riders are not going fast, but they must be able to control the bikes with their bodies.

slalom—a downhill race in which riders weave through sets of poles
maneuver—to make planned and controlled movements that require practiced skills

CHAPTER 7

How to Get Started

Freeriding and other motocross sports are a great way to get outside and experience natural beauty. The sport has a wide variety of skill levels. This means it is possible for young riders to get involved early, with the right safety precautions. The biggest decision is finding the right bike. The AMA uses a guide based on age to determine the proper size and power of bike. Parents should help young riders select the correct size, and all bikes should be tested before riding.

Beginning riders should wear as much protection as possible. Minor crashes are likely as new riders work on their skills. Having the proper helmet, padding, goggles, boots, and other safety equipment will help prevent serious injury. Before young riders start attempting big jumps or tricks, practicing basic bike skills is necessary.

A new rider should practice starting, stopping, and safely getting on and off a bike.

Many local motorcycle shops will have information about groups for beginning riders. Joining a club is a good way to learn how to safely operate a bike. Experienced riders can also offer tips and techniques to make riding easier and safer. Some areas also have bike parks, which are great places to practice.

There are many steps beginners can take to improve their skills. Working with the clutch and brakes will give riders an idea of the bike's limits. Practicing proper body position can help with jumps. Young athletes can ride in circles and figure eights to learn how to lean and master bike control. These are all skills the best moto riders have learned with years of practice.

Motocross is a great way to get outside and spend time with friends. Take it slow and keep practicing. Racing for the checkered flag could be in your future!

Glossary

agility (uh-GI-luh-tee)—the ability to move fast and easily

checkpoint (CHEK-poynt)—a place along the route of a long-distance race where the time for each competitor is recorded

ciruit (SUHR-kuht)—a series of races that leads to a single championship

cylinder (SI-luhn-duhr)—a hollow area inside an engine in which fuel burns to create power

dab (DAB)—the act of a rider touching the ground with their foot for support

finesse (fuh-NES)—great skill or style

format (FOR-mat)—the shape or style of something

maneuver (muh-NOO-ver)—to make planned and controlled movements that require practiced skills

obstacle (OB-stuh-kuhl)—something that gets in the way or prevents someone from doing something

regulation (reg-yuh-LAY-shuhn)—an official rule

slalom (SLAH-luhm)—a downhill race in which riders weave through sets of poles

strategy (STRAT-uh-jee)—a careful plan or method

suspension (suh-SPEN-shuhn)—a system of springs and shock absorbers used to suspend a vehicle's frame, body, and engine above the wheels

terrain (tuh-RAIN)—the physical features of a piece of land

torque (TORK)—a force that produces or tends to produce rotation

traction (TRAK-shuhn)—the gripping power that holds a vehicle's tires to the ground

READ MORE

Doeden, Matt. *Dirt Bikes*. North Mankato, MN: Capstone Press, 2019.

Lainer, Wendy Hinote. *Dirt Bikes*. Lake Elmo, MN: Focus Readers, 2017.

Perritano, John. *Motocross Racing*. Vero Beach, FL: Rourke Educational Media, 2015.

INTERNET SITES

American Motorcyclist Association: Racing
https://www.americanmotorcyclist.com/Racing/Story/beginners-guide-to-motocross-1

Motoworld
https://www.motosport.com/blog/motocross-kids-dirt-bike-racing

Red Bull: Motocross
https://www.redbull.com/gb-en/how-to-start-motocross-riding

INDEX